SPOTLIGHT ON GEORGIA

GEORGIA DURING RECONSTRUCTION

SAM CROMPTON

PowerKiDS press

NEW YORK

Published in 2018 by The Rosen Publishing Group, Inc.
29 East 21st Street, New York, NY 10010

Editor: Melissa Raé Shofner
Book Design: Michael Flynn
Interior Layout: Reann Nye

Photo Credits: Cover, pp. 7, 13, 17, 21 Everett Historical/Shutterstock.com; pp. 5, 25 Courtesy of the Library of Congress; pp. 7, 13, 15, 21, 23, 25 Reinhold Leitner/Shutterstock.com; p. 9 https://commons.wikimedia.org/wiki/File:Graves_Hall,_Morehouse_College_2016.jpg; p. 11 Marzolino/Shutterstock.com; p. 15 Bardocz Peter/Shutterstock.com; p. 18 Time & Life Pictures/The LIFE Picture Collection/Getty Images; p. 19 https://commons.wikimedia.org/wiki/File:First_Colored_Senator_and_Representatives.jpg; p. 23 Historical/Corbis Historical/Getty Images; p. 27 Hulton Archive/Getty Images; p. 29 Kean Collection/Archive Photos/Getty Images.

Cataloging-in-Publication Data

Names: Crompton, Sam.
Title: Georgia during Reconstruction / Sam Crompton.
Description: New York : PowerKids Press, 2018. | Series: Spotlight on Georgia | Includes index.
Identifiers: ISBN 9781508159810 (pbk.) | ISBN 9781508159841 (library bound) | ISBN 9781508159827 (6 pack)
Subjects: LCSH: Reconstruction (U.S. history, 1865-1877)--Georgia.
Classification: LCC F291.C76 2018 | DDC 305.896'073075809034--dc23

Manufactured in the United States of America

CPSIA Compliance Information: Batch #BS17PK For further information contact Rosen Publishing, New York, New York at 1-800-237-9932.

CONTENTS

CHAPTER ONE

TIMES OF UNCERTAINTY

The Civil War ended in the spring of 1865. Robert E. Lee surrendered to Ulysses S. Grant, and the surrender of other Confederate leaders followed. Georgia, and the South in general, lay in ruin.

Less than a week after Lee's surrender, President Abraham Lincoln was **assassinated**. This meant the **Radical Republicans** in Congress could push their plan of making the South pay for its actions. What followed was more than 10 years of back and forth between politicians. There were two big questions at the time: How should the South be rebuilt? And what roles would blacks and whites play in the process?

White Georgians were upset over losing the war. Black Georgians were happy to have won their freedom but uncertain about what would happen next. Like other Southern states, Georgia had to wait to see what the federal government would decide.

The Civil War caused great damage throughout Georgia. The state faced many questions about rebuilding when the war ended in 1865.

CHAPTER TWO

LINCOLN'S RECONSTRUCTION PLAN

Toward the end of the Civil War, President Lincoln announced his objectives for the former Confederate states. He knew the North and South needed to forgive each other, and he wanted them to do so quickly.

In 1863, Lincoln announced his "Ten Percent Plan." This plan stated that when 10 percent of a state's residents had declared their loyalty to the Union, the state would be readmitted. Lincoln wanted to make things easy for the South so the Confederacy would surrender and Reconstruction could begin. With the Ten Percent Plan, he hoped to create peace between the North and South. To further emancipation, or the freeing of slaves, Lincoln's plan required Southern states to create new governments. These new state governments would need to rewrite their constitutions to abolish slavery. It was Lincoln's hope that Southern states would return to the Union with new governments that were loyal to his plan of emancipation.

On January 1, 1863, President Lincoln issued the Emancipation Proclamation, which declared slaves in the Southern states to be free. Despite this declaration, the Civil War continued. Lincoln used his Ten Percent Plan to push for a quick, peaceful resolution to the war.

CHAPTER THREE

THE FREEDMEN'S BUREAU

In March 1865, Congress established the Freedmen's Bureau to provide housing, food, legal help, and more to former slaves and poor whites in the South. One of the main goals of the bureau was to help blacks transition from slavery to freedom. It was the first social welfare organization in the United States. The Freedmen's Bureau also concentrated on education, particularly for blacks. By 1871, the bureau had helped found 11 black colleges and universities. By 1868, bureau teachers had taught thousands of former slaves how to read.

The Freedmen's Bureau had a fair amount of success, but in Georgia, limited funding resulted in slow progress. Congress had never planned the bureau to be a permanent institution, and it was shut down in 1872. During its short time, the Freedmen's Bureau changed the lives of thousands—perhaps hundreds of thousands—of people in Georgia.

The Freedmen's Bureau supported the foundation of several black colleges. Morehouse College in Atlanta, Georgia, is a private, all-male, historically black college founded shortly after the Civil War ended.

CHAPTER FOUR

PRESIDENTIAL RECONSTRUCTION

Vice President Andrew Johnson became the new president after Lincoln was assassinated in 1865. Johnson wanted to restore the Union quickly, and his Reconstruction plan was similar in many ways to Lincoln's.

Johnson was against the rich Southern plantation owners, but his actions made it seem otherwise. His Reconstruction plans often tended to favor them, which was the opposite of what the Radical Republicans had been hoping for. Johnson also believed former slaves shouldn't be given the same rights as whites. Many Northerners felt Johnson's Reconstruction plans went too easy on the South. They believed many of his policies worked against what the North had fought for during the Civil War.

In the 1866 election, Radical Republicans hugely defeated the Democrats, which started a period of Radical Reconstruction. In 1868, with many people still angered over his Reconstruction policies, Johnson became the first president to face **impeachment** by the House of Representatives.

President Johnson's impeachment trial came to an end when the Senate failed to meet the two-thirds majority vote needed to remove him from office.

CHAPTER FIVE

THE 13TH AMENDMENT

Almost as soon as the Civil War began, there was discussion about how to amend, or change, the U.S. Constitution. The Constitution is the supreme law of the United States and originally allowed slavery to exist.

The 13th Amendment is brief and to the point. It abolished, or ended, slavery in the United States. Naturally, many former slaveholders disliked this. Former slaves wanted more, such as citizenship and voting rights. It was clear that further legal and constitutional steps were required.

As part of President Andrew Johnson's plans for Reconstruction, any Confederate state that wanted to rejoin the Union needed to first adopt the 13th Amendment. Georgia was the 27th and deciding state to adopt the amendment, which officially became part of the U.S. Constitution in December 1865.

The U.S. Senate passed the 13th Amendment on April 8, 1864. Thirty-eight senators (pictured above) voted for the amendment and six voted against it.

CHAPTER SIX

CONGRESSIONAL RECONSTRUCTION

After the 1866 elections, the Radical Republicans took control of the U.S. House and Senate. Led by Thaddeus Stevens of Pennsylvania, they planned to punish the South for its actions in the Civil War with more force than Johnson had.

In 1867, Congress passed the First Reconstruction Act, which divided the former Confederate states into five districts. Military units were stationed throughout the South to protect former slaves and help keep the peace. Georgia's state constitution had to be rewritten, and the state was first readmitted to the Union in 1868. Unfortunately, problems in the area continued and the Union put Georgia back under military control. Georgia was readmitted to the Union again in 1870.

During this period of Congressional Reconstruction, a number of African Americans were elected to local and state government positions. In Georgia, the three most notable state legislators were Tunis Campbell, Aaron A. Bradley, and Henry McNeal Turner.

When Congress divided the former Confederate states into districts, it also declared martial law. This meant the state governments were powerless and the military was in charge. Georgia, Alabama, and Florida made up the third military district.

CHAPTER SEVEN

A NEW FORM OF WHITE SUPREMACY

The Ku Klux Klan (KKK), a **white supremacist** group, was established in Tennessee in 1866. In Georgia, John B. Gordon, one of the state's most notable military and political figures, served as a KKK leader. First founded as a social organization, the Klan turned into a political one. It is perhaps the most **dangerous** organization of its kind in American history.

Former Confederate general Nathan Bedford Forrest turned the Klan in its new direction. Klansmen, wearing white robes and hoods, terrorized African Americans, usually under the cover of night. Klan members wished to scare blacks to prevent them from voting or running for office.

Over time, the Klan became even more **aggressive**, seeking to block any attempt at social equality. In the early 1870s, the federal government began to make a strong push against the KKK. The Klan soon weakened, and most of its leaders headed into hiding.

This drawing from *Harper's Weekly* (February 24, 1872) shows Ku Klux Klan members pointing a gun into the home of an African American family.

CHAPTER EIGHT

HENRY MCNEAL TURNER

One of Georgia's most influential black leaders at this time was Henry McNeal Turner. Turner had never been a slave, and he was educated. These were uncommon **circumstances** for an African American in the South at this time. Turner was a preacher in the African Methodist Episcopal Church. This role took him to Washington, D.C., where he became friends with several important Republican legislators, including Thaddeus Stevens.

In 1867, Turner helped organize Georgia's Republican Party and was elected to the Georgia House of Representatives. His time in office was cut short in 1868, when white legislators removed black legislators from their political positions.

HENRY MCNEAL TURNER

FIRST AFRICAN AMERICAN SENATOR AND REPRESENTATIVES

Jefferson Long (top right) was Georgia's first African American congressman. Long's political career was greatly influenced by Henry McNeal Turner. The two men worked together on several projects.

In response to this, Turner delivered a remarkable speech to the Georgia House of Representatives on September 3, 1868, demanding black legislators' rights. Turner regained his position in 1870 but failed to be reelected just a few months later.

CHAPTER NINE

THE 14TH AMENDMENT

The 13th Amendment ended slavery. However, it didn't end the unfair treatment of African American workers. In 1865 and 1866, Georgia and other Southern states passed laws called Black Codes. These laws limited the types of jobs freedmen could hold. They also made it legal to whip black workers as punishment.

To fight back against the Black Codes, Congress passed the Civil Rights Act of 1866, which gave African Americans citizenship. To build on this act, Congress passed the 14th Amendment in July 1868.

The 14th Amendment promises citizenship to anyone born in the United States. It also promises equal protections for these people under the law. The amendment was created with the rights of freed slaves in the former Confederate states in mind. Since then, it's been used for the protection of many people.

Joint Resolution proposing an amendment to the Constitution of the United States.

Article XIV.

The 14th Amendment officially gave freed slaves U.S. citizenship. It promises equal protection under the law for all citizens regardless of race, religion, or age.

CHAPTER TEN

POLITICAL NAME CALLING

In the late 1860s, two new terms arose in Georgia politics: scalawags and carpetbaggers. During and after the Civil War, many Northerners headed to the South with the desire to make more money. Southerners often believed these people wanted to take advantage of the problems in the South for a profit. These Northerners became known as carpetbaggers. Despite this nasty nickname, some carpetbaggers actually did mean well and wanted to help freed blacks. Some, however, were truly just in it for the money.

Some white Republicans in the South were called scalawags. Though many were against rights for blacks, they felt that supporting Reconstruction and giving former slaves more rights would be beneficial to them. Scalawags made up about 20 percent of the white electorate. They were seen as traitors to the South for not favoring the traditional views of white supremacy.

Carpetbaggers and scalawags supported the Radical Republicans' plans for Reconstruction. In Georgia, the government had more scalawags than carpetbaggers. Republicans in Georgia sent many of the state's scalawags to Congress.

CHAPTER ELEVEN

THE 15TH AMENDMENT

When Ulysses S. Grant was elected president in 1868, the Radical Republicans saw an opportunity. They wanted one more amendment to the Constitution. They were most concerned with the rights of freed slaves living in the former Confederate states.

Congress passed the 15th Amendment in February 1869. Three-fourths of the states then needed to approve it, and Georgia was second to last among those that gave their approval. The 15th Amendment was ratified, or approved, in February 1870, and Georgia reentered the Union that same year.

The 15th Amendment gave African American men the right to vote. It states that voting rights can't be denied based on a citizen's race, color, or history of slavery. With ratification of the 15th Amendment, many Radical Republicans declared their work done. They had done everything in their power to ensure that slavery no longer existed.

The 15th Amendment gave African American men the right to vote, but Southern states continued to **disenfranchise** them using reading and writing tests, poll taxes, and other methods.

CHAPTER TWELVE

SHARING THE CROP

In the 1860s, many Southern landowners and **tenants** worked out agreements in which the tenants farmed the land and crops grown there—usually cotton and tobacco—were divided between the tenants and owners. This system was called sharecropping.

Over the next decade, many Southerners established sharecropping agreements. Typically, a landowner provided tools and seed to sharecroppers, who lived on and farmed the land in exchange for up to one-third of the total crop. This system kept many sharecroppers poor and without land of their own. Sharecroppers were not always former slaves. In fact, about two-thirds of all sharecroppers were poor whites and about one-third were former slaves.

Sharecropping is often confused with tenant farming. The two systems are similar but have one major difference. Unlike tenant farming, sharecropping involves little, if any, exchange of money. Instead, crops act as **currency**. Sharecropping remained an important part of Georgia's economy well into the 1900s.

The workers pictured here are planting sugar cane in Georgia in the late 1860s, when the sharecropping system began.

CHAPTER THIRTEEN

THE NEW SOUTHERN ECONOMY

Many Northern congressmen hoped the Southern economy would undergo great change during Reconstruction. For the most part, however, this didn't happen. There were a few changes in coastal Georgia, where products made from pine trees became an important new industry. The textile, or fabric, industry also grew at this time.

The interior of the state relied on the same products as before, with cotton, wheat, and corn continuing to be important crops. However, cotton was now being grown in many other parts of the world, so it was no longer Georgia's main crop.

As late as 1890, most Georgians worked on farms and in industries similar to those their parents had known. Former slaves mostly did the job of picking the cotton. They were now free men, but their lives looked a good deal like they had before.

After cotton was picked and separated from its seeds using a cotton gin, it was placed into a cotton press such as the one shown here. Mules or horses would turn the cotton press, which would compress the cotton into **bales**.

CHAPTER FOURTEEN

RECONSTRUCTION IN REVIEW

Reconstruction was an attempt to remake the social and economic structure of the former Confederate states. Unfortunately, the economy now relied heavily on sharecropping and tax rates increased. There were some successes, however. Thanks to the constitutional amendments made during Reconstruction, former slaves had rights in the eyes of the federal government. African Americans were now U.S. citizens. African American men had the right to vote and could run for political office. The Freedmen's Bureau was also successful in some ways, especially in educating former slaves.

After Georgia was readmitted to the Union, many white Georgians acted as if nothing had happened. They continued on with their lives as if the world remained as it was prior to the Civil War. However, many Georgians, both black and white, felt let down. The economy and social structure of Georgia still needed a lot of work.

GLOSSARY

aggressive (uh-GREH-siv) Acting with forceful energy and determination.

assassinate (uh-SA-suh-nayt) To kill someone, especially a public figure.

bale (BAYL) A large, tight group of objects tied together.

circumstance (SER-kum-stans) A condition or fact that affects a situation.

currency (KUR-en-see) Money.

dangerous (DAYN-jeh-rus) Able to cause harm.

disenfranchise (dis-ehn-FRAN-chyz) To keep a group from a legal right or privilege, especially the right to vote.

impeachment (im-PEECH-ment) The act of charging a public official with a crime done while in office.

Radical Republican (RA-dih-kuhl rih-PUH-blih-ken) A branch of the Republican Party from the Civil War era that was made up of people who were completely opposed to slavery and wanted to grant equal rights to freed slaves.

tenant (TEH-nint) A person who rents land from a landowner.

white supremacy (WYT suh-PREH-muh-see) The belief that white people are better than those of other groups.

INDEX

PRIMARY SOURCE LIST

Page 5
Ruins of a railroad depot in Atlanta. Photograph. George N. Bernard. Atlanta, GA. 1864. Now kept in the Library of Congress Prints and Photographs Division, Washington, D.C.

Page 17
"Visit of the Ku-Klux." Wood engraving. Drawn by Frank Bellew. From *Harper's Weekly*. February 24, 1887. Published in New York, NY.

Page 25
"The Fifteenth Amendment." Watercolor print. Thomas Kelly. ca.1870. Now kept in the Library of Congress Prints and Photographs Division, Washington, D.C.

WEBSITES

Due to the changing nature of Internet links, PowerKids Press has developed an online list of websites related to the subject of this book. This site is updated regularly. Please use this link to access the list: www.powerkidslinks.com/sog/recon